MW00659300

Student
DISCUSSION GUIDE

to

Touching Spirit Bear

By Ann Maouyo

Talent Development Secondary
Center for Social Organization of Schools
Johns Hopkins University
Baltimore

Discussion Guide #1

Chapters 1 - 6

Vocabulary List A

defiantly (p. 3)
skiff (p. 3)
omen (p. 3)
banishment (p. 3)
wisecracking (p. 3)
*humility (p. 4)
smirked (p. 4)
chafed (p. 5)
*feigned (p. 5)
remote (adj., p. 6)
cowering (p. 7)
resented (p. 8)
prosecutor (p. 11)
wallow (v., p. 14)
winced (p. 14)
reluctantly (p. 15)
grudgingly (p. 15)
shrouded (p. 16)
moseyed (p. 16)
brandished (p. 20)
revoked (p. 22)
smoldered (p. 22)
fantasized (p. 22)
*ignited (p. 22)
*mustered (p. 23)
shimmering (adj., p. 24)
spewing (p. 24)
barrage (p. 24)
venomous (p. 24)
inferno (p. 25)

The Writer's Craft

"In Medias Res"

"In medias res" is a Latin phrase meaning "in the middle of the thing." This is a term coined by the Roman writer Horace, who lived in the first century B.C. It describes a way of telling a story that has been around even longer than that – the practice of beginning in the middle of a difficult or suspenseful situation, then going back to fill readers in on the events leading up to that situation. The technique is very popular in the "drama in real life" stories in popular magazines. The article begins with the main character in some exciting, challenging, or dangerous situation. Then the writer goes back to tell us how the character came to be in that situation. Finally, the story explains how the character resolves the problem or escapes the danger. You can find examples in magazines, television shows, and movies.

continued...

This novel begins with the main character, Cole Matthews, on his way to an uninhabited island where he is to spend a whole year alone. This situation sparks our curiosity because it raises many questions. *Why is Cole going to live on the island? Who are the men taking him there?* For the first six chapters, the story goes back and forth between the "now" of Cole's stay on the island and the "before"– his memories and **flashbacks** of events in his life that brought him to this point. Read carefully to make sure you understand the order in which the events of the story actually occur.

DISCUSSION QUESTIONS AND ACTIVITIES

Section I. Read chapters 1 and 2. Discuss your responses to the questions and activities with a classmate. Then write your answers separately.

1. **Describe Cole Matthews. What have we learned about his family life?**

2. **Describe the incident in which Cole injured Peter Driscal. How are the consequences of this incident different from those of previous arrests?**

3. **Who is Garvey? What does he tell Cole about Circle Justice? Why does he give Cole the at.óow?**

4. **Tell about Edwin, the third person in the boat. Why does he make Cole wear his clothes inside out? Why did he go to so much trouble to prepare for Cole's stay on the island?**

5. **Describe Cole's attitude toward Garvey, Edwin, and the trip to the island. What is he feeling as he sets the shelter on fire?**

Make A Prediction:

How will Cole survive on the island now that he has destroyed his shelter and his supplies? What will Edwin and Garvey find when they return in a couple of days? How will they react?

Vocabulary List B

stifling (adj., p. 27)
wearily (p. 30)
ricocheted (p. 30)
billowing (adj., p. 30)
devoured (p. 30)
hysterical (p. 30)
engulfed (p. 30)
*subside (p. 31)
manic (p. 32)
frigid (p. 32)
scoffed (p. 33)
arraignment (p. 36)
symbolizes (p. 38)
*obligations (p. 38)
*illusion (p. 41)
flailed (p. 42)
lurking (adj., p. 44)
massive (p. 44)
mangy (p. 44)
taunted (p. 47)
rigid (p. 48)
muted (adj., p. 49)
intently (p. 49)
unflinching (p. 49)
*persistent (p. 52)
vegetation (p. 52)
scrounged (p. 53)
coaxed (p. 53)
quest (p. 56)
*skepticism (p. 56)
bristled (p. 57)

The Writer's Craft

Dialogue

A **dialogue** in a work of literature is a conversation between two or more people. The tone of a dialogue and the words used by each character give readers a new understanding of each character's personality. In addition, writers use dialogue to provide insight into background events related to the main story. The next section contains many sections of dialogue in Cole's memories of events leading up to his banishment on the island. As you read, think about about what these sections of dialogue reveal about Cole, about his parents, about Garvey, and about Peter Driscal and his family.

DISCUSSION QUESTIONS AND ACTIVITIES

Section II. Read chapters 3-6 (pages 26-57). Discuss answers to the following questions with a classmate, then write your answers separately.

1. **How did Cole explain his anger about life to Garvey? What do we learn from Garvey's response?**

2. **Why did Garvey make Cole eat the different cake ingredients before giving him a piece of cake? What point was he making? What do we learn about Garvey, and about Cole, from this incident?**

3. **Describe the positions taken by Cole's parents at the first Hearing Circle. How did Cole, Garvey, and the Keeper of the Circle respond?**

4. **Identify the main concern expressed by Peter's mother and his lawyer. How did this lead to Cole's banishment to the island?**

5. **Describe Cole's plan for escaping the island. What goes wrong with this plan?**

6. **How does Cole react to seeing the white bear on the island? What do you think of his attitude at this point in the story?**

Make A Prediction:

Will Cole succeed in escaping from the island on his second try?

Literature-Related Writing

1. Pretend you are the Keeper of Cole's Hearing Circle. How would you feel after its first meeting? What concerns would you have? Write a brief **report** based on the account given on pages 35-40 and 46-52.
2. Everyone makes wrong choices sometimes. Think back to a wrong choice that you made. What were the consequences? Did facing the consequences help you to make better choices afterward? Why or why not? Write a **personal narrative** telling about your experience.
3. Pretend you are Garvey. What hopes and fears would you have after leaving Cole on the island? Write a **journal entry** describing your feelings and concerns.

Extension Activities

1. Use Internet or library resources to learn more about Circle Justice. Report what you learn to your class.
2. "Spirit Bears" are members of the black bear species that happen to be white. Research the life and habits of black bears. Present an oral report to your class, or create a poster to share your discoveries.

3 Draw a picture or create a diorama to represent an island scene from the story (for example, the cabin Edwin made, Cole's escape attempt, or his sighting of the Spirit Bear).

Discussion Guide #2

Chapters 7 - 13

Vocabulary List A

*passive (p. 59)
maggot (p. 59)
charred (p. 59)
sapling (p. 59)
craving (n., p. 60)
roiled (p. 60)
*turbulent (p. 60)
receding (p. 60)
eerie (p. 60)
scavengers (p. 61)
pelt (v., p. 62)
incessant (p. 63)
*makeshift (p. 63)
rivulets (p. 64)
boulder (p. 64)
conceding (p. 64)
deflected (p; 65)
gluttonous (p. 68)
*brazenly (p. 68)
mauled (p. 69)
tentative (p. 70)
wracked (p. 71)
*haphazard (adj., p. 75)
stuporous (p. 76
pummeled (p. 77)
sensation (p. 77)
detonated (p. 77)
acrid (p. 77)
insignificant (p. 78)

Special Glossary

orca whale - (*also called* “killer whale”) a large black dolphin that hunts in packs

fetal position - a position in which one curls up into a tight ball (so called because it is the position of a fetus in its mother’s womb before birth)

northern lights - a band of unusual, curtain-like green or red lights that appears near the horizon in the night sky in northern latitudes (also called the *aurora borealis*)

The Writer's Craft

Irony

Irony is a word used to describe a situation where what really happens is very different from what one might have expected-for example, when the cartoon character Wile E. Coyote is caught in the very trap that he himself set to catch Bugs Bunny. Watch for an ironic situation in the next chapters.

Epiphany

The word **epiphany** was originally used in a religious context to mean a revelation or vision of God in an everyday setting. However, it has also come to be used as a literary term to mean a character's sudden, unexpected insight or realization of some deep personal or spiritual truth. Epiphanies can be the result of an experience of great beauty or great suffering - or just a new way of seeing something very ordinary.

In this section, Cole Matthews has an epiphany. Watch for it as you read, and ask yourself, *What brings Cole to this point? What does he suddenly realize? What evidence indicates to readers that a major change has taken place in the way Cole views his life?*

DISCUSSION QUESTIONS AND ACTIVITIES

Section I. Read chapters 7-9 (pages 58-79). Discuss answers to the following questions with a classmate, then write your answers separately.

1. **Page 60 describes Cole's state of mind as "... empty. There was no beauty." List some of the unusual things Cole had seen that day (pages 58-60). Why do you think he has no reaction to them?**

2. **Why and how does Cole plan to kill the Spirit Bear? Do you think this is a good idea? Explain.**

3. **List the physical injuries Cole receives as a result of attacking the Spirit Bear. Describe his condition when the bear goes away.**

4. **What reminds Cole of Peter's injuries after Cole beat him up? Why does Cole believe the two situations are different?**

5. **What is ironic about Cole's situation, and about his reaction to it?**

6. **Describe Cole's epiphany. What shows us that his way of looking at life has changed?**

Make A
Prediction:

What will happen to Cole? If he survives, what other changes will we see in his attitude?

Vocabulary List B

doggedly (p. 80)
grimacing (p. 80)
frail (p. 82)
fragile (p. 82)
*squandered (p. 84)
hallucination (p. 84)
convulsed (p. 85)
dislodged (p. 85)
ejecting (p. 85)
grueling (adj., p. 85)
quarry (p. 88)
*replenish (p. 89)
forage (p. 91)
intense (p. 92)
sauntered (p. 93)
exposed (adj., p.93)
penetrated (p. 94)
*resigned (adj., p. 95)
meager (p. 95)
*bizarre (p. 98)
bombarded (p. 98)
gibberish (p. 98)
haggard (p. 100)
*commotion (p. 101)
delirium (p. 101)

Special Glossary

medivac - (*short for* "medical evacuation") helicopter or small plane used to transport people from remote areas for urgent medical care

hypothermia - (*medical)* an excessively low body temperature

The Writer's Craft

Symbolism

A **symbol** is a physical object that is used to represent something that is not physical, such as an idea or an emotion. For example, a flag symbolizes a nation or a group of people, while a mascot serves as a symbol for a sports team or perhaps a school. A wedding ring is a symbol of the love and commitment shared by a couple when they marry.

These are public symbols recognized by many people. However, people also have private symbols–for example, you might feel that a watch that your grandfather left you symbolizes your family heritage. In this novel, Garvey gave Cole the at.óow as a symbol of trust. What change do you see in Cole's attitude toward the at.óow in the next section? What do you think this tells us about what is happening in Cole's life?

DISCUSSION QUESTIONS AND ACTIVITIES

Section II. Read chapters 10-13 (pages 80-112). Discuss answers to the following questions with a classmate, then write your answers separately.

1. **List things that Cole forces himself to eat in order to survive. How do you think this affects the way he feels about life?**

2. **How does Cole feel when the Spirit Bear returns? What differences do you notice, compared with his earlier attitude?**

3. **How does Cole feel when he believes that his life is over? Why can this moment be considered a second epiphany?**

4. **At what point in the story did you realize that Cole was being rescued? At what point does Cole realize it? What do you think he means when he repeats to Garvey, "I *am* okay" (page 102)?**

5. **What does Garvey tell Cole about his reasons for helping him? What does Cole learn about the probable consequences of his choices on the island?**

Make A Prediction:

How will Cole's parents react when they learn what has happened? Will he have to do time in jail?

Literature-Related Writing

1. Cole's experience on the island changed in his thinking at a very deep level. Have you ever had an epiphany that changed your whole outlook on life? Write a **personal narrative** describing your experience. Explain what brought about your epiphany, how it changed you, and how it continues to affect your life today.
2. Pretend you are Garvey. Write a **report** of what happened to Cole on the island. Include your suggestions for what should happen to Cole when he is released from the hospital.
3. Write a **poem** about a thunderstorm or another amazing event in nature. (Note: The poem does not have to rhyme.)

Extension Activities

1. Create a work of art, such as a drawing, painting, or collage, illustrating Cole's dramatic experiences on the island.
2. With some classmates, select a portion of chapter 13 to act out as a skit. Present your skit to the class.

Discussion Guide #3

Chapters 14 - 20

Vocabulary List A

hobbled (p. 115)
orbs (p. 116)
stark (p. 118)
*relinquish (p. 119)
monotonous (p. 120)
reverently (p. 124)
indifferently (p. 126)
*diminished (p. 126)
instinctively (p. 127)
*traumatic (p. 128)
sarcastically (p. 129)
*inevitable (p. 130)
frenzy (p. 131)
irked (p. 134)
canopy (p. 135)
retrieving (p. 136)
potential (n., p. 137)
wry (p. 137)
savoring (p. 139)
warily (p. 143)
*vulnerable (p. 145)
uncontrollably (p. 145)
fester (p. 146)

Special Glossary

gunwales - side edges of a boat

bow - front of a boat (*rhymes with* "cow")

DISCUSSION QUESTIONS AND ACTIVITIES

Section I. Read chapters 14-17 (pages 115-146). Discuss answers to the following questions with a classmate, then write your answers separately.

1. **How do Cole's mom and dad behave when he returns to Minneapolis? What does Cole learn about his family background?**

2. **How do the participants at the Circle Justice meeting feel that Cole's case should now be handled? What is the point of Edwin's demonstration?**

3. **How will Cole's new exile on the island be different from the first one? How does Cole feel about the new conditions?**

4. **Garvey and Edwin like to illustrate their life lessons using tangible physical experiences. The chart below lists two of those experiences. Fill in the blanks, summarizing the lesson that each example illustrates.**

Illustration	Teacher	Lesson Being Taught
The hot dog feast (pages 138-139)		
The ends of a stick (pages 144-146)		

5. **What do you think Edwin means by "breaking the left end of the stick to get rid of their anger"? Give a practical example.**

Make A Prediction:

How will Cole build the shelter?

What will Edwin and Garvey's dance be like? Will Cole dance too?

Vocabulary List B

*sheepish (p. 149)
*deliberately (p. 150)
*gingerly (p. 150)
stoked (p. 150)
tarp (p. 152)
waterlogged (p. 152)
ancestors (p. 154)
*redemption (p. 157)
solitary (p. 158)
loped (p. 158)
stammered (p. 160)
wavered (p. 160)
momentarily (p. 163)
dawdled (p. 165)
caulking (v., p. 169)
conjuring (p. 171)
trance (p. 171)
hypnotic (p. 172)
regained (p. 173)
composure (p. 173)

Special Glossary

breaching - (*of whales or dolphins*) leaping out of the water

The Writer's Craft

Conflict

Every story includes **conflict**–problems or tensions that must be resolved. Conflict can occur between two or more characters; it can also occur between a character and nature, or within a character (for example, a character who is trying to break a bad habit, or make a tough decision). As you read the next section, notice the different types of conflict that Cole faces. Which conflict do you think is the most important one in the story?

DISCUSSION QUESTIONS AND ACTIVITIES

Section II. Read chapters 18-20 (pages 147-176). Discuss answers to the following questions with a classmate, then write your answers separately.

1. **What triggers Cole's anger as he begins work on the shelter? How does he express his anger?**

2. **Why does Garvey tell Cole that they will be returning to Minneapolis the next day? What effect does this announcement have on Cole's attitude and behavior?**

3. **In the chart below, list some of the things Cole learns from his dances and the early morning activities that Edwin taught him. Why do you think Garvey decides that he can stay on the island after all?**

Activity	**Lesson Learned**
Whale dance (pages 151-152)	______________________________
Wolf dance (pages 161-162)	______________________________
Soaking in the pond (pages 163-164)	______________________________
Carrying the rock (page 165)	______________________________
Rolling the rock away (page 166)	______________________________

____

____

____

____

____

____

____

4. **Why do you think Edwin and Garvey have Cole act out dances based on different wild animals? How can this help him change his life?**

5. **List some of the conflicts that Cole faces in this section. Which do you think is the most important conflict?**

Make A Prediction:

What will happen to Cole after Garvey and Edwin leave?

Will he see the Spirit Bear again?

What is the "one thing" that Edwin says Cole needs to discover in order to heal completely (page 175)?

Literature-Related Writing

1. Pretend you are Cole. Write several **journal entries** from different points in time in this section. Make sure your journal entries reflect Cole's changing concerns, frustrations, hopes, and fears during this period.
2. Garvey and Edwin care enough about Cole to be strict with him when necessary. Is there someone in your life whose "tough love" has helped you to grow as a person? Write a brief **character sketch** of this individual.
3. Using library or Internet resources, research the humpback whale or the gray wolf. Write a brief (one-page) **report** presenting your discoveries.

Extension Activities

1. How much would it cost to build a small shelter like the one Cole will live in on the island? Make a list of materials needed based on the descriptions found on pages 148 and 159. Sketch the floor plan on graph paper and calculate the quantity required of each material. Visit a hardware store in person or online and estimate the total cost of the project.
2. Make a small scale model of Cole's shelter, or a diorama of the pond where he and Edwin go to soak in the mornings.
3. Choose a wild animal that you believe has valuable life lessons for you. Create a dance representing that animal's character or behavior. Present the dance to your classmates. Explain what you learn from the animal you chose.

Discussion Guide #4

Chapters 21 - 28

Vocabulary List A

groggy (p. 179)
bouts (p. 182)
*ingenuity (p. 186)
deformed (p. 186)
*meandered (p. 190)
stalked (p. 193)
writhed (p. 193)
fester (p. 196)
*treacherous (p. 198)
*confined (adj, p. 198)

Special Glossary

thermals - rising columns of warm air that eagles and other large birds use to reach greater heights in the sky

DISCUSSION QUESTIONS AND ACTIVITIES

Section I. Read chapters 21-24 (pages 177-205). Discuss answers to the following questions with a classmate, then write your answers separately.

1. **Cole finds a big log near the shoreline. What ideas come to his mind about ways to use it? What is his final decision, and how does he reach it?**

2. **Why does Cole want to be "invisible"? What does he decide is the secret to being invisible?**

3. **List some of the important actions that are part of Cole's anger dance. How does the dance end?**

4. **According to Edwin, what does Cole need to find in order to heal?**

5. **What is happening to Peter? What does Cole think might be a way to help him?**

Make A Prediction:

How will Edwin respond to Cole's suggestion?

Will Peter agree to come to the island? If he does, what will happen?

Vocabulary List B

plodded (p. 208)
rehabilitation (p. 213)
quivered (p. 214)
*confronted (p. 228)
*maneuvered (p. 229)
dumbfounded (p. 232)
sledgehammer (p. 236)
*ambled (p. 238)

Special Glossary

trawler - a fairly large motorized boat, such as those used in commercial fishing

The Writer's Craft

Climax and Denouement

The **climax** of a story is the moment at which the conflict reaches its highest intensity–which is also the turning point leading to a resolution of the conflict. What is the main conflict in this part of the novel? At what point does it reach a climax in this section?

The word **denouement** (day-noo-MANH) refers to the resolution of the conflict. What is the denouement of this novel? What details indicate that the main conflict is indeed on its way to being resolved?

DISCUSSION QUESTIONS AND ACTIVITIES

Section II. Read chapters 25-28 (pages 206-240). Discuss answers to the following questions with a classmate, then write your answers separately.

1. **What measures are taken so that Peter's parents feel comfortable leaving him on the island with Cole? Why do they decide to return to the mainland after just two nights?**

2. **How does Peter express his feelings about Cole? How does Garvey encourage Cole not to give up on helping Peter?**

3. **What is the first sign that Peter is beginning to open up? How does his anger toward Cole come out in the open?**

4. **How does bringing a pole to camp for Peter to carve improve the relationship between Peter and Cole?**

5. **Why do you think Peter suggests going to the pond alone with Cole? In what ways does this prove to be a breakthrough for the boys?**

6. **By what actions do Cole and Peter symbolize their decision to forgive?**

Literature-Related Writing

1. Edwin says that he and Garvey "lived on the phone" for the two weeks they were planning Peter's stay on the island. What do you think they discussed? Write a **dialogue** of a conversation Edwin and Garvey might have had when Edwin first told Garvey about Cole's suggestion that Peter come and stay on the island.
2. Pretend you are Peter. Write several **journal entries** or a **letter** that Peter might have written to his parents during his stay on the island with Cole and Garvey.
3. Have you ever become friends with someone who had previously been your enemy? Write a **personal narrative** about your experience. Explain why and how this person was your enemy, and what happened to change your relationship to a friendly one.

Extension Activities

1. With a parent's permission, make a carving out of soft wood or another material, such as soap. Show your carving to your class.
2. Research one of the animals mentioned in this section, such as the beaver, salmon, raven, or mouse. Make a poster or give an oral report to share what you learn with your classmates.
3. Create a drawing to illustrate this section, or design an original book jacket for the novel.

53429750R00023

Made in the USA
San Bernardino, CA
16 September 2017